KEEPER OF MY SOUL
TESTIMONIALS

Look What God Has Done!

FIRST EDITION

Printed in the United States of America

ISBN: 0-9910218-0-0
ISBN-13: 978-0-9910218-0-2

DEDICATION

In Honor of my Heavenly Father, my Lord and Savior

TABLE OF CONTENTS

ACKNOWLEDGMENTS

When God tells you to do something, you should listen to Him. Because we are human, we have the nature of self-doubt. When God laid this project on my heart, I too had doubts. I called everyone close to me for their opinions, but what they gave me was God's confirmation.

Mrs. Lisa Levine (my step mother whom I love as if she was my birth mother) said, "You are a very good writer and that sounds like a good idea. Others need to know about the miracles of others."

Evangelist Ida Balloue (my Morning Dew partner and dear friend) said, "Pray about it and let God lead you. God will tell you what to do; He will never tell you to do something that is outside of His will."

I told them all about my desire to one day write a book, but I feel like God is leading me to create something that everyone can take part in. We all have a testimony that can help someone else. I hear them every day, and God gave me the desire to want to put them together in devotional form for all to read.

EVERYONE SAID, "GO FOR IT!!"

I would like give a special thank you to my earthly father, Mr. James E. Levine Sr. Without his love, encouragement and support in my life, I would not be the woman I am today! Thanks Daddy for always being there for me when I really needed a shoulder to lean on!

INTRODUCTION

YOU ARE NOT ALONE.

There are times in our lives when we think we are alone and no one knows what we are going through. There are many others going through the exact same trials, tribulations, hurts, heartaches and pain as you are. Continue to read the "Testimonials" in this book and be uplifted by the Miracles God has performed in the lives of others. Be assured that what He's done for them, He can do for you.

Psalm 37:3-5

Trust in the LORD, and do good; so shalt thou dwell in the land; and verily thou shalt be fed, Delight thyself also in the LORD: and he shall give thee the desires of thine heart. Commit thy way unto the LORD; trust also in him; and he shall bring it to pass.

Undivided Attention

On September 23, 2011, I was sent home from Afghanistan. At the time, I had been with my company for 3 plus years. I climbed the corporate ladder at record-breaking speed. Within my first six weeks of employment I went from a worker bee Logistician to Lead Logistician ending, with the job title of South West Asia (SWA) Lead Logistician over three countries (Iraq, Kuwait and Afghanistan). I went from $106, 000.00 dollars to $266,000 dollars by the end of my third year. I was the ONLY female Supervisor and I am an African American.

During the month of August, 2011, my company was pressed to move out of Iraq; where I had spent six years. My husband (who worked for me at the time) was leaving Iraq before me. Being the Supervisor, I was one of the last to leave. In the process of the packing and moving, a clear plastic zip lock bag was found. Due to a photo of me being clearly visible in the bag, it was assumed to be mine. I told the gentlemen who brought the bag into my office that it wasn't mine. My husband quickly spoke up and stated the bag was his. Well, due to him leaving later in the day, he asked me to mail the bag for him. Of course I said, "Yes." A few days later (when time permitted) I took the bad to the camp post office. During the clerical inspection of the contents of this bag, two CD's marked "SECRET" were discovered. The post office Supervisor was called over. He explained to me that he would be calling the Military Police (MP) and I could not leave the post office. (It is a crime to mail secret materials to a United States residence.) I tried to explain to the Post Office Supervisor that we were packing up and the CD's probably got there by mistake. The CD's were from 2006 and clearly outdated. The bag was not mine. It belonged to my husband and I was simply mailing it. I didn't feel the need to search the bag because I trust my husband. I was trying to explain the situation with the truth. Needless to say, they were NOT hearing it. The MP arrived at the post office some 30 minutes later. He asked me about the CDs and I told him the same story I had told the post office Supervisor. He asked me if I had a Carrier's Card, which allows me to carry and handle Secret materials. I told him, "Yes I have one." He checked my credentials and returned the CDs to me and I left. I'm thinking "No harm No Foul" right; but I was wrong. The post office Supervisor was NOT happy. I then took the CDs to my boss and told him what happened. He placed the CDs into his computer to verify the contents and deemed the CDs FOUO (For Official Use Only), not SECRET. I told him he may be contacted concerning the incident. He told me they had until the next day to contact him because he was leaving for Afghanistan at that time. He took the CDs and cut them up with a pair of scissors. He was not contacted and I thought it was over.

One week later, I was told I had 48 hours to leave the country. I was stripped of everything: security clearance, ID cards, computer access and pride. I was suspended without pay, but allowed to go on medical leave due to a prior injury. I came home hurt, angry and depressed. After all I had done for them (my company and the military) this is how they repaid me. I was barred from the three countries I supervised and wrote Standard Operating Procedures and Policies for. I was blacklisted by the people I thought were my friends. It was as if I never existed.

After arriving home, I sought medical attention for my arm. In my heart, I knew I had to have surgery; the two cortisone shots I had during the prior year only lasted a few months each. During this time, I had this bright idea to get my bunions fixed at the same time. I figured since I'm out on medical leave I can kill two birds with one stone, so I sought medical treatment for that as well.

The surgery to have my left foot bunion fixed was October 18, 2011; it went fine. The surgery for tennis elbow was November 1, 2011; it too was a success. The surgery for my right foot bunion was December 6, 2011; this is where everything changes. I noticed on December 9, 2011, my pain was excruciating. The doctor told me I was expecting too much too soon. A month went by and I was still in pain. He told me I had a hematoma (pool of blood) under my foot and sent me to physical therapy. Oh my God, I thought I was going to lose my mind; the pain was so intense. I decided to get a second opinion. It turns out the first doctor cut the tendon that operates my big toe during my bunion surgery. To add to my dismay I was faced with another surgery.

Let's tally this up...I have no job, medical problems and I am alone for the most part. My husband is in Afghanistan, my children are grown and my closest family is an hour and a half away. (My Mama Lisa did come spend a week with me each time I had my bunion surgeries). But (ultimately) I felt alone.

On February 14, 2011, yes Valentine's Day I was in the hospital getting my tendon repaired in my right foot. I would rather have 10 babies without anything to numb the pain than have another foot surgery. My second day out of the hospital is when God started talking to me. I had been reading the daily devotional from Antioch Missionary Baptist Church for a little while now. It has become a part of my life; reading it every morning makes me happy. What I didn't know was God was getting ready to do some things in my life. On this second night from the hospital my pain was so intense I remember calling on Jesus three times, saying, "Jesus, Jesus, Jesus please let me go to sleep just for a little while. And please take the pain away." I fell asleep directly thereafter. Lisa (who was in bed with me) said she asked me if I was alright? I didn't hear her. I was asleep! God is Good Amen!

I recalled these events with Lisa the next day and told her how God let me rest. Well, Lisa went home a few days later; God really started talking to me. He said, "Now I have your attention...do you remember the last time I had your undivided attention?" I said, "Yes, Lord! It was the end of 2004, the beginning of 2005." He spoke further to me revealing why I was where I was at this point in time. He said, "I blessed you and you forgot about me. When you were unemployed and didn't know how you were going to pay your bills and feed your children, I sent you overseas, I promoted you and your cup was running over. Not once did you acknowledge me. Everything was I (meaning you) and not Glory to God your Lord and Savior; so I had to knock you down to get your attention."

My God, the light bulb came on inside my brain. I could see all my sins, mistakes and faults. After my revelation God also told me, I will bless you again, but first there are some things I want you to do.

I have been listening, obeying and working for the Lord for only a few months. I can say I have a JOY and Peace unlike no other. I am happier than I've ever been in my life. God only wanted me to acknowledge Him for ALL He had done for me. I don't plan to make that mistake ever again. I have put God First in My Life!!

I still have some pain in my right foot, but I have elected not to have another surgery unless the pain becomes unbearable. God has blessed me to return back to work in Kuwait. This job is better than my last one. This job allows me to spend all the time I want with God. Thanking him for a husband who stood by me and supported me financially. Thanking Him for family and friends that were there when I needed them. Thanking Him for HIS favor, grace and mercy. Thanking Him for just being GOD!

-- Tina Levine

Psalm 103 – Bless the Lord O my soul and FORGET NOT all His benefits.

Will You Be His Witness?

The year was 1984. I was a military wife. A mother of a 9-month-old daughter. We were stationed in Stuttgart, Germany. To all outside appearances, we had it all. Staff Sergeant husband, beautiful apartment, money in the bank, a loving relationship. Momma always told me, "Never judge a book by the cover." As a young person, that statement never meant much to me. I thought it was just a cliché the old folks used. My husband was simply handsome. The man had a beautiful personality, charm, and was fun to be with. I had married my friend, my lover, the man of my dreams.

Behind closed doors though, I quickly realized the man he presented to the public on the outside was not the man on the inside. See, behind closed door my husband was an alcoholic, an abuser both mentally and physically, a workaholic, and a cheater. Through many tears I wondered, How did I not see this man? I prayed and asked God, "What did I do at twenty one years of age to deserve this HELL I now found myself in?" I asked the Lord, "When will it end?" I even prayed to God for Him to take my life. I didn't see a way out. I didn't have a job; no money of my own. He controlled all our finances. I even prayed that God would let him have an accident and be killed.

One Saturday morning after a long night of beatings, cursing and destruction of our home, my husband left the house early that morning. As always, I began to clean up the mess because those were my instructions before he left: "You better have all this cleaned up before I get back home." Through tears, my mind screamed HOME! This is NOT A HOME! It's a nightmare. So with a busted lip and bruises covering me, I went about cleaning up broken glasses, broken dishes, and picking up clothes thrown out of the closets. "Lord," I prayed, "IF you are real, IF you can hear me, HELP ME!"

Later on that morning there was a knock at the door. There stood two woman, one black and the other one white. They asked me if they could have a few minutes of my time. They were on the Evangelical team from Patch Chapel Fellowship Church. I invited them in. One of the women asked me if I had accepted Jesus Christ as my personal Savior. I grew up in a small church. When I was growing up we had to participate in every activity the church had to offer. It was not an option. We were taken to Sunday school, Bible study, prayer meeting and children's choir rehearsal. Yet, I did not have an answer for this woman's question. I'm beat-up, hurting physically and mentally. I'm discouraged and depressed. Lady, I don't understand what you're asking me. I NEED HELP NOW! Her next question was, "Will you allow us to pray for you? Are you willing to give your life to Jesus?"

"Yes," I said. You know, when your world has caved in and your back is up against the wall and there is NOTHING left, you will do anything for peace in your soul. I was familiar with the Bible and I was desperate. "Yes," I said again. Both women held my hands. I was trembling and scared. I didn't know when my husband would return home. With a pocket Bible they read from the scripture Romans 10:9-10. I accepted Jesus to come into my life. They invited me to Church and said, "We will come pick you up on Sunday."

No matter where you are, Jesus will meet you. Even in Stuttgart, Germany. That was 28 years ago. No, the beatings did not stop. Within five months my husband was discharged from the Army. Within two months after his discharge and much prayer and fasting, I was on my way home to Louisiana. At 27 years old, as a single mother with no job, no income of my own I was moving back home with my 103-year-old grandmother. The spirit of the Lord spoke to me in prayer and gave me this promise Psalm 37:25 I have been young, and now I'm old; Yet have I not seen the righteous forsaken, nor his seed begging bread. Thank you Jesus.

Since that day, there have been many mountains and

valleys. There have been times of doubt and times of great joy. There have been miracles. But through it all I've never left Jesus out of my life. I've never forgotten those two women and their obedience to God to go and witness for Him.

In a foreign country on foreign soil, two women knocked on my door and proclaimed the love of Jesus. They spoke words of encouragement in my life that God had not forgotten about me. Today I am an Evangelist, imparting the love or Jesus and witnessing every chance I get. Today I am a college graduate. Today my daughter is a senior at Stephen F. Austin University in Nacogdoches, Texas. God is Faithful. We were not left begging bread. Hal-le-lu-jah, Jesus. I can minister with an assurance. Woman of God, you can survive. You will be His Witness to His Power and His Protection. There is No Distance from God to you.

Stuttgart, Germany was a turning point in my life. Thank you, Jesus, for those two women who ministered to my soul. When I thought all hope was gone, on foreign soil, in a foreign land, you used them to be Your witness just for me.

Will you be His witness??

-- Evangelist Ida Balloue

Lamentations 3:22-23 – It is of the Lord's mercies that we are not consumed, because His compassions fail not. They are new every morning: great is thy faithfulness.

Journey to Forgiveness

Most young people go through that stage when all they think about is where the next party is, or what's happening this weekend. The summer before I turned 18, I was drinking every night and neglecting every dream or ambition I had before to go to college and become a nurse. All I cared about was a boy, my friends and my next drink.

This one particular night, I was upset because my first boyfriend and I had parted, we were at the same party and he was flirting with other girls. I don't even remember what I was drinking. All I know is that I had a large cup and I didn't let it go the whole night. I had a friend bring me home; the whole evening is nothing but a dark haze with snapshots of what happened to me that still to this day play over and over in my head. I was raped by two men in my own home, in my own bed. One of them I once considered my friend. He hung out at my house with my other friends plenty of times before.

This guy who I had once considered my friend, brought another friend along and they both had their way with me. When I woke up the next morning I was half dressed, bleeding and in severe pain from the top of my head down to my legs. The fear of the unknown and the shame that ran through my whole entire soul had me glued to the bed. I refused to move, I was paralyzed with fear, because they were still there... one of them sound asleep next to me like everything was okay. The one that I had once considered my friend was talking to my little brother, nonchalantly telling him that they had spent the night, were about to go, and to, "Tell your sister I said 'bye.'" This is the point I had to choke back tears; they made it seem so normal. So, I immediately started to blame myself. I must have given him some kind of signal. Maybe I don't remember giving consent. This has to be my fault.

I was angry at myself. I was angry with God and those

guardian angels I thought would always surround me. I retreated into myself. Before long, my Mother sent me to live with my Grandmother. I had ruined her house with all the partying and I had neglected my little brother. He was basically raising himself. My Grandmother is a sweet woman, but she can also be tough and cold at times. So, I kept it to myself. I kept it to myself for a few years. I became very promiscuous, like I didn't care about myself anymore. I didn't realize until now it came from lack of self-esteem. I thought I was being powerful and womanly taking control of my body and who could have it. I was only hurting myself. Then when men became old and I no longer wanted to entertain myself in that way, I started drinking a liter of vodka every day. I would get wasted until I couldn't function anymore and I would just pass out on my couch. I was lonely and alone. I was self-medicating and severely depressed.

On a normal day just like any other, I was driving through my apartment complex and I saw the man I had once called a friend outside playing with his daughter. I burst into tears and asked God, "Why are you letting this happen? I just want to forget about it and pretend it never happened, so why is he here?" I live in the next building over from the man who raped me. I thought of all the evil things I could do, like spray paint "rapist" across his truck, slash his tires, and throw a brick through his living room. But he has a daughter and I would never cross the line like that when children are involved. As soon as my lease was up, I moved. I was running away from this "thing" that had been haunting me for years.

Last year it was February of 2011. I was sitting at my kitchen table and I grabbed a pen and paper. I started writing. I wrote the best way I knew how... I wrote a poem. I admitted to that piece of paper and to myself what had happened to me. I released myself from all blame because it wasn't my fault. I did not ask for what happened to me to transpire. I did nothing wrong. Then this voice—I didn't know if it was my voice, God's voice or an angel comforting me—but it said, "Now, let it go. Forgive him. Forgive yourself and let it go."

I felt so good afterwards and my spirit was lighter! My breakthrough came when I wasn't even expecting it. I was going to live with what had happened to me for the rest of my life and just cope. That's no way to live, though. When someone does something wrong to you, forgive them. I'm not at all excusing people when they do something horribly wrong, but when you hold onto that anger it eats YOU up inside, and that person is going about his or her life probably not thinking about you. So, let it go and live the blessed life that God has planned for you.

-- P. Jay, Houston, TX

1 John 1:9 – If we confess our sins, HE IS FAITHFUL and just to forgive us our sins, and to cleanse us from all unrighteousness.

CYPHER PUBLISHING, LLC

God's Got My Back

As a pre-teen I was very curious about church. God was something we never talked about in my home. Luckily, over the years I had friends who went to church and I was able to go with them. I never understood it, but would go just to get out of the house. At the age of 12 I went to a church camp with my grandparents and got saved. I think I got saved only because I knew it was expected of me, but I still didn't really understand. As I grew I had this hunger, but I didn't know what to with it. I could never find a church I was comfortable in.

In May of 2000 I went with my boyfriend to his church where his uncle preached. It was the first time I ever felt a connection. It was like the preacher had made this sermon about my life and was only talking to me. I remember only having five dollars to my name and I gave it to the church because I had been told that God will not let you go without. To my surprise God did not let me down.

Fast-forwarding to October 2007, I went to church with another boyfriend; this time I cried during the whole sermon. I could feel the words and I felt the Lord's presence. I finally felt like I had found a church home. I can't explain why I never felt any connection in a white church, but in black churches I am touched to my very soul. Now don't get me wrong, I still didn't understand, but I wanted to do good in the eyes of God.

In September 2011, I had questions concerning my life. Where I am going to be? What will I be doing? I gave myself a time line. Nothing was going according to my plan. I was so stressed and angry all the time. I finally stepped back and apologized to God. I told him I was sorry for thinking I could do this all on my own. I put my life and my future into His hands and told Him I would travel whatever path He put me on. I asked Him to remember I was a single mother and to please take care of me and my son. As soon as I did this, all the weight I had been carrying was gone. A few months before I had signed up for section 8, but the waiting list was three years long. About seven months after I signed up, I got a letter in the mail saying my name had come to the top of the list for low income housing. Guess what? I didn't even know I was on this list!! Three weeks later I had my own apartment! God is great!

After graduating college I had to stay home and take care of my newborn. I started interning at an office to get some experience. My contract ran out, but suddenly I was hired at another place. God is great! It's only temporary, but I'm getting experience and I'm networking. I also know God has my back, so I'm not worried.

Lately, I have been having issues with my car. God is great! Now, why am I saying God is great when something bad is happening? Because I have learned that God has His hands on everything and I'm thankful! Yes, my car is breaking down, but I have a job that will allow me to pay for getting it repaired! I had to learn to see a positive in everything and that everything happens for a reason. I'm still learning and I can't quote scriptures, but I know God loves me and as long as I do my part God is going to always have my back!! God is GREAT!!!

-- Angie Allen

Jeremiah 29:11 – For I Know the plans I have for you, says the Lord. They are plans for good and not for disaster, to give you a future and a hope.

Small Miracle

I don't really know how to pray. I feel silly doing it, actually, but I would do anything for my child. My husband of seven years decided to not pay our electric bill in the middle of winter in order to have more money to hang out with his friends. I didn't know this until I woke up one morning and I was freezing. Our electricity was turned off. My irresponsible husband was of no help when I called the electric company, begging and pleading for them to turn it back on... My three-year-old child and I were in the cold.

I paid what I could out of my own pocket, but we still owed a measly forty dollars. The tears were streaming down my face as he was telling me there was nothing else they could do. I had to pay them. As I got off of the phone, I sunk to the floor in the middle of my kitchen and I started talking to God. Not for me, not for my stupid husband, but for my innocent child who needs heat in the middle of the winter. How was I going to cook for him? How was he going to take a warm bath? I was so desperate. I cried and I prayed until I couldn't speak anymore.

When I opened my eyes, my baby was standing there with his socks in his little hands. I put them on for him and I just held him really tight. I told him it was going to be okay; of course, I was really telling myself that. We started playing in the living room and about an hour later... everything in the apartment came to life! All I could do was cry. My baby said, "Mama crying?" I said, "It's okay baby, I'm happy because God heard me."

Something so small meant the world to me. My electricity coming back on was probably a mistake on someone else's part, but God made a way when I couldn't see. I will be eternally grateful for that small miracle.

-- Anonymous

1 Peter 5:7 – Give all your worries and cares to God, for he cares about what happens to you.

How Long Should You Carry the Pain?

I was 10 years old the first time my mother said she hated me. As a child, my only choice was to hate her back. I could not understand why my mother felt this way. She said it was because I looked and acted like my father. As a child, I thought this was a badge of honor; I loved my father deeply and thought he was the only person in the world who loved me.

I wasn't born perfect like my mother's sons. I was born with a hemangioma also known as a blood tumor. I had heard rumors of there never being a bond between us when I was an infant because she thought I was a birth defect. I felt as though this was the real reason she hated me. I don't know this to be true or false, but I know there was never a bond there. I never asked my mother about the events of my birth; she was only 16 when I was born, and at this point those details really don't matter.

My mother spent most of my childhood in night clubs. Her favorite was Club 21. I spent from age seven to ten being molested by my grandmothers' boyfriend on my mother's side. Even if she believed me, she did nothing to protect me. My father spent my childhood fathering other children. There was no one to care for me! The children, including my own brothers, teased me because I have a nasty-looking scar on my neck. The names I was called will never be forgotten because they deeply hurt me. There was no love anywhere for me.

The relationship with my mother has always been difficult. As a young teen, I used to fantasize about having a close mother-daughter relationship with her. I would see it on television or in some families in my neighborhood. I knew mothers and daughters who had difficulty relating to one another. This was nothing new to me. I think it is super special when mothers and daughters have a close bond. The second time my mother told me she hated me, I was 15 years old. I decided to run away with the first boy who told me I was pretty. I don't recall all the details of the day, but what I do remember is being smart-mouthed with my mother, and she slapped me across my face. My grandmother, her mother, had to intervene. I knew that day I would leave and never return.

My mother and I have spent the last 35 years at odds with each other. We would go years without speaking to one another for various reasons. Something significant had to happen to someone, such as severe illness or death in the family, before we would speak or see one another again. I do recall that each time we started to speak again, I had to initiate it.

As a young adult, I tried to buy my mother's love. I bought her jewelry, clothes and even gave her money. As long as I was doing things for her I was a "good daughter," but when I could no longer do those things I became a B----- again. I spent a lot of time being told I was useless and would never amount to S---. My father once told me no matter what I did, I could never buy my mother's love. It was at that moment I stopped trying.

After devoting my life to Christ, I felt like this part of my life was yet unresolved. I attend church regularly and I would hear the sermons, but it is not until you give your heart to God and ask Him to heal it of all past pain that you realize how long you have been holding on to a certain pain. God works in mysterious ways. The lack of love my mother was able to give me really affected my life. In some ways it was positive, and in other ways it was negative.

The positive impacts on my life have been: I gained independence, I am strong and successful. I used all her negative talk as fuel every time I wanted to quit something. I dropped out of high school after the 9th grade, but later joined the military and graduated college Summa Cum

Laude with a 3.8 GPA. I was always book smart. Every time I wanted to give up I could hear her voice saying, "You will never amount to S---!" So, I would just press on. I did all this while working a full time job, with three children and being a single parent.

The negative impacts on my life have been: I didn't know how to love. I looked for love in all the wrong places. I've had four husbands and many failed relationships before I figured out that I had to first love myself! I wanted my mother's love, but didn't love myself. My first husband was a physical abuser and a cheater. My second husband was an emotional abuser, physical abuser and a cheater. My third husband was an inmate at a prison I worked at. My forth husband was an emotional abuser and a cheater. There was no love anywhere for me. I didn't know how to love. I didn't have a role model in this department as a child. My mother hated me and Papa was a rolling stone, but God's grace and mercy kept me!

In July 2012 I invited my mother out to lunch. I wanted to establish some sort of relationship with her. She accepted and then she cancelled on me. I invited her out a second time; she accepted, then cancelled on me again. Well, I told God I had enough I was NOT inviting her out again. God had been speaking to me concerning my feelings towards my mother, so I asked God to work it out for me. I do know that once God works something out, it is well worked out.

In the midst of God working it out I decided to write her a letter:

Hello Mom,   *August 21, 2012*

I pray that you receive this well. I am not sending this to you to hurt you or make you angry. It's just something you need to know.

Even as an adult, what I perceive as your "lack of love for me" still hurts me to my heart and down through my soul. I cried today because of it. I have made several attempts to see you, "Just You," wanting to spend a couple of hours just looking at your face. Hoping to see the beautiful smile I rarely saw as a child, but remember clearly. I know the mother-daughter relationship I longed for as a child is long gone. However, I still long for the smallest measure of love I can get from you. It truly broke my heart for you to cancel on me yet again.

You traveled more than an hour to see a dead man whom you have not seen in 30 or more years, but cancel constantly on the daughter who's right here longing to see her mother. I'm sure you are saying, "Well, you could come to my house." As I stated previously, "I want you all to myself!" "By myself!" You have many distractions at home – husband, children and grandchildren. They have you all the time; I only want a few hours.

I'm sure you may not think so, but I do love you. You are my mother...differences aside, you will always be my mother.

If I have offended you, I am sorry. It was never my intent. God is working on me and I will get there. I simply wanted to share with you what is in my heart.

You really never actually know how your actions affect others until they tell you. My heart is broken and my soul can't stop crying!

I love you Always and Forever,

Your Daughter

I never got the opportunity to mail this letter. When I gave this to God, He worked it out this way. I didn't have her mailing address and when I called to get it from her, she invited me out to lunch. I accepted and I told her most of what was in the letter, and she received it well. We don't have that close mother-daughter bond, but we do at least have a cordial relationship and talk at least once a week. God is Good!!

-- Anonymous

Matthew 11:28 – Come unto me, all ye that labour and are heavy laden, and I will give you rest.

CYPHER PUBLISHING, LLC

Love is Love

They say, "Great things happen when you least expect it." It is also said that even better things happen to those who wait. Seems cliché to add this too, but remember the song lyrics, You can't hurry love, no, you just have to wait. They say love doesn't come easy, it's a game a give and take. I listened, I did wait, and something great did happen. I met a wonderful person who has changed my life in more ways than one. Here is how it all began.

We met in September 2012, just hanging out in the garage of a mutual friend while sharing mutual interests; music and laughter. At the time, I was interested in someone I met a few months before. It so happened that the person of interest lived in another state, which made things quite difficult for the both of us. Despite the distance and the lack of trust, I remained loyal and respectful. I made a great effort. I really was determined to move out of town to be with him and to pursue my career where he lived.

As it unexpectedly resulted, all it took was meeting a new person one day... and the sparks flew. Let's call him SB. It was a Wednesday afternoon when I pulled up into my friend's driveway and walked to the front door. There he was, opening the door and welcoming me in with his respectful gentleman charm and a bright smile. I sensed so much positivity and calmness. It was refreshing. I entered the garage and greeted my friend with the usual kindness. SB offered me his seat and stood by as he made every effort to attend to every need I might have had. I was taken aback. I never met anyone so attentive and generous. I was intrigued. Although I was intrigued by him, I did let him know I was talking to someone. He respected it. But something told me to get to know him. So I did. It took me a few days to finally call him, but I did. We conversed for about an hour or two and we seemed to get along really well. We agreed to meet at the local park the following morning so we could exercise. Thankfully, it all went really well. We shared a few funny stories and made a commitment to maintaining healthy lifestyles. Another day to exercise was chosen.

SB and I continued to hang out as friends, but we were both developing feelings for each other. Eventually I had to tell the person I had interest in that I was seeing someone else. He was disappointed but, I could not help how I was feeling. I fell for someone when I least expected it. He is everything I have ever wanted and more. Someone kind, attentive, thoughtful, determined, creative, funny, family-oriented, understanding, and loving. I can say I am blessed. Being patient really did pay off.

-- Anonymous

Psalm 138:8 – The Lord will perfect that which concerns me. Your mercy and loving kindness, O Lord endure forever, forsake not the works of your own hands.

1 John 1:3 – And truly our fellowship is with the Father, and with his Son Jesus Christ.

Submit your own testimonial at:

www.morningdewisyourbreakthrough.com/
keeper-of-my-soul-testimonials

Recommended website:

MORNING DEW IS YOUR BREAKTHROUGH

Our mission is to encourage all believers to make a commitment to start their day with prayer and the reading of God's Word. Because of our shared belief and knowing that others have made the commitment to begin their day with the Lord we will become empowered to face the challenges of the day, strengthen our spirit and be obedient to the word of God.

Psalm 5:3
"My voice shalt thou hear in the morning, O LORD; in the morning I will direct my prayer unto thee, and will look up."

Learn more about Morning Dew Is Your Breakthrough at www.morningdewisyourbreakthrough.com

Prayer Pillows Now Available!